COLDHARBOUR

PREVIOUS BOOKS BY
KATHRYN DASZKIEWICZ

In the Dangerous Cloakroom, Shoestring Press, 2006
Taking Flight, Shoestring Press, 2012
A Book of Follies, Shoestring Press, 2017

COLDHARBOUR

KATHRYN DASZKIEWICZ

Shoestring Press

Printed by imprintdigital
Upton Pyne, Exeter
www.digital.imprint.co.uk

Typesetting and cover design by The Book Typesetters
hello@thebooktypesetters.com
07422 598 168
www.thebooktypesetters.com

Published by Shoestring Press
19 Devonshire Avenue, Beeston, Nottingham, NG9 1BS
(0115) 925 1827
www.shoestringpress.co.uk

First published 2022
© Copyright: Kathryn Daszkiewicz
© Cover artwork: 'The Lovers' card from 'The Crow Tarot'
created by MJ Cullinane

The moral right of the author has been asserted.

ISBN 978-1-915553-15-7

ACKNOWLEDGEMENTS

Acknowledgements are due to the editors of the following publications and websites where some of these poems first appeared: *Acumen, Brittle Star, The Frogmore Papers, The High Window, Orbis,* and *Quartet: The Four Seasons* (Avalanche Books, 2018.)

In memory of Rebe and Bill Wallace

CONTENTS

Harm and the Man   1
Tam Lin   3
Mistletoe   4

Three Poems Inspired by the Paintings of Edward Coley Burne-Jones
I The Myths We Make our Own.   5
II The Depths of the Sea   8
III Laus Veneris   10

Summer's End   11
Four Seasons of Haunting   12
Meres Knoll   13
The Apple Tree on Inner Street   14
Eternity Spent   15
Murmuration   16
The Lone Turnstone   17
Wings   18
Nowhere to Hide   19
Underbrush   20
Cuckoo Pint   21
Coldharbour   22
Love's Elastic   23
A Year and a Day …   24
Living in the Moment   25
GINNEL   26
    (i) The Space Between   26
    (ii) Collage   26
    (iii) Rib   27
    (iv) The Lovers   27
    (v) … and the Wardrobe   28
    (vi) Silver   28
    (vii) Being Watched   29
    (vii) Seventy-seven Steps   30

Cuckoo Spit   31
Wayward   32

The Lost Art of Patience   33
The Plague Doctor of Hellesdon   34
The Aunt Who Never Was   .   35
Visiting Time   37
   (i) Short Back and Sides   37
   (ii) Losing It   37

Sharing a Ride   38
Pathetic Fallacy   39
Lammastide   40
The Names of Grasses   41
The Greenwood Speaks: Twelve Trees of Ogham   42
  Birch   42
  Rowan   42
  Alder   43
  Willow   43
  Ash   44
  Hawthorn   44
  Oak   45
  Holly   46
  Hazel   46
  Apple   47
  Ivy   47
  Elder   48

Woods Seen from a Train   49
Losing the Plot   50

.

HARM AND THE MAN

That bone
skimming my flesh
as I reach for you mid-
fall
    is called
the ilium.

Too close to the surface
of your skin

it must have been cold
and you quite starved

as you hunkered among echoes
and the scent of resin
in the belly of the horse.
Alert for
an opening.

This time
after such an absence

there are no
burning towers

only a woman
who is reduced
to watching you

vanish

even as you come

close

but does not run from
the treachery

of your
dwindling arms.

TAM LIN

Such an unquiet place you are
in sleep; a shift, a twist
a gasp – as if you're
going under.

A gentle palm
laid on the broad
sail of your pitching back
won't steer you
to a calm.

I need to get a grip –
like the Scots maid
in that tale

who holds on
tight as flesh
translates
                            to beast
                    to newt
                        to snake
                            to bear
                                to hot iron bar

breaking the spell
to ferry you across

that liminal space
the bridge between your demons
and a dawn.

MISTLETOE

I passed an oak on a winding country lane
a clot of mistletoe lodged in its branches –
cross section of my head.
My head which once
was such a sacred space.

Forget the kissing, the deep green smell of holly
the writhe of ivy garlands and the wine.
Berries like frosted pearls, but as intrusive
as grit that forms the round inside the shell.
Something that agitates. An irritant. A parasite.
An alien in the chamber.

The Doctor of Physic confides to Macbeth
he has no art to pluck a rooted sorrow
out of the brain. And even now, it cannot be dissolved –
only allayed by something in a glass
or blister pack.

The oak's a royal tree. I'll take a hook to it.
Hang it above that doorway into hell
where fires still burn.

Three Poems Inspired by the Paintings of Edward Coley Burne-Jones

I THE MYTHS WE MAKE OUR OWN.

(i)

It hung over my bed like a prophecy,
The Tree of Forgiveness – a woman, rooted in,
but leaning from her carapace of bark
to clasp the faithless man.
The soft clash of limbs ...
the horror on his face
... recoil in every muscle
as he twists.

Behind, a mocking spread
of almond blossom
all froth and lace and scent.

Certain paintings, he said, followed him
like an old sin.

He stayed away too long,
Demophöon. The myth
diverges. Does Phyllis
slip the noose
around her neck or do the gods
transform her?

Some things are beyond scolding –
hurricanes and tempests
and billows of the sea ...

Was there a casket
which concealed a sign?
Did he embrace the trunk on his return
and wake her spirit?

What's in his eyes is fear.

(ii)

Born at the foot of Olympus,
her name burned like strong liquor
on his tongue. *She looked and was primeval.*

Zambaco stares from canvas after canvas
as Circe, Venus, Psyche, Nimue. Clutching
white dimity. *Love Among
the Ruins.*

Phyllis bears her face,
her snaking hair.
Demophöon, his own.
*I don't know why
I've such a dread of lust.*

He went along with plans
to flee to Greece.
The staid wife
found a note.
He couldn't leave.
And rued the Puritan
taint in English blood.

Drowning or opium?
A pact skewed to one side.
A struggle on the towpath. And an end
of sorts. *Love and his
overdriven steeds...*

(iii)

I discover much too late
lines from *Heroides*
the painter knew by heart:

Mihi, quid feci, nisi
non sapienter amavi?

Tell me what I have done
other than love unwisely...

II THE DEPTHS OF THE SEA

The friends who found
the print had thought it an apt gift –

a woman buoying up a sinking man
but being dragged down herself.

Perhaps they missed
the curving mermaid tail.

His calm expression,
serene as the Hanged Man

on a Tarot card,
could have misled them.

Victim or venerist?
Saint, sinner or seductress?

The ambiguity
is all.

Her siren-eyes are dreamy
but she pins his arms

in a caress of steel.
Grey pillars loom –

a frozen moment
in a fluid tale

where they descend,
his lungs redundant,

between the stonework
into the dim recesses

of the deep
salt water womb:

a prison
or deliverance

where he,
out of his element,

can slip forever
from the curse of choice.

III LAUS VENERIS

It was the playing away that gave it frisson.
But then the net came down. And there they were.
Exposed. A laughing stock.
It just so happened that the cuckold
was a god at metalwork.

Now she reclines in a flame-orange gown –
bored with the music that's about to play,
bored with the colourless knights
who ogle through the window.

If you move right in close,
the need to break the rules – to run your fingers
over gold stitching overlaying the silks –
is urgent as an itch. The paint is in relief.

A lesson learned, she wears as ornament
that delicate chain link. Armour which keeps
at bay what, if it's never spent,
cannot devalue like crude currency.

The memory of that combat is too raw.
The peacock fan's discarded on the floor;
she knows now not to be seduced by show.

SUMMER'S END

We dug into the flesh
and in the skin we carved us
each a face

a nose and eyes and lips
then gave it fire

bringing the dark to life
to free our shadow selves.

When you had gone
I found a single seed upon the sheet
that spoke of transformation

a gilded coach that flew across the moon
reverting to a gourd.

Alone, I keep that little of your essence
and the vague disquiet it brings

but there's a potency
in being the one who's left

all barefoot in the hearth
sifting the still warm cinders
through her hands.

FOUR SEASONS OF HAUNTING

When someone's placed a branch
of yellowing oak with scarlet
hips and haws into a jar

or when he sees a pumpkin lantern stare
from a dark window-ledge at witching hour

when coal fires burn in out-of-the-way inns
mulled cider on the air

when nodding grasses nudge between
the cracks of his Prozac-tidy life

or when that wild flower
whose name he can't recall
spills from a sun-warmed wall
as the opening notes of 'In Between Days'
waft from a radio

he'll find a dandelion seed head on his coat,
a tiny parachute which floated from
the clock she blew
one lazy afternoon

find he's in free fall
to that sometime past
he forfeited
and there's no

land in sight

MERES KNOLL

The song you gifted me is raw.
I follow the slow track
but the lines that led to straying now hang slack.

Were you mere catalyst? I couldn't
free myself without a fall.

I cross a stream
dammed with thrown stones and sticks
to slither down a slope and mount the stile
into the cemetery.

I see a grave that bears my maiden name –
the moth-like lightness of it turned to stone.

Those wings I spun to rise
from the cocoon are lying limp
beside a crushed flat-pack.

What's joined together second time around
is always loose. There is no
going back.

THE APPLE TREE ON INNER STREET

No one has picked a single apple
from the tree on the corner of Inner Street
weeping gold into the gutter.

Fruit for the taking... No gilt except
the sun-glow of its skin.
Unwrapped, organic –
just one pluck away.

No dragon's coiled around the trunk.
But that streak of brightness from one laden bough
conjures the deft stroke of divinity
that fires a thousand canvases
where pent-up Danae lies.

A barrel's bobbing on a swelling ocean.
A bribe, a theft ... the launching of a fleet.

Angels still chase
the ones who dare to taste –
from paradise
into a dying world.

ETERNITY SPENT

                without you

would be like Eden
minus the snake – the only fire
coming from the sun.

An earth that didn't move. No fall
of man or leaves. The same
green always.

Constellations without name,
only promising more
of the same.

Find me knee-deep in bracken
(that will never rust
or crackle) dying

to be
stung back
into life.

MURMURATION

How did each one know how to glide –
forward or back or to whichever side
across the sky this January dusk?

On second-guessing wings
they swerved and turned in time
fluid, as one – they moved in rhyme

so synchronised it seemed absurd.
Who'd guess, at dark,
that we could be as birds?

THE LONE TURNSTONE

left the quick pickings of flat rocks at low tide
his tortoiseshell summer colours
on the turn.

The sea wind over the Black Midden rocks
dispersed the warning of his skirling cry

as far as the velvet beds
and the site of that lost village near the bay

to cormorants on a stack
their blacks sun-greened

and Lizard Point
where the defunct lighthouse stood
striped in Sunderland colours

past the grey stone wall
where the linnet
sang at dawn.

On reaching Potter's Hole

he made the break
(*interpres* – go between)

before the cold set in.

WINGS

"The more materialistic science becomes the more angels I shall paint: their wings are my protest in favour of the immortality of the soul."
– Edward Burne-Jones to Oscar Wilde

Not flimsy, or transparent, but robust
and muscular, like those of giant birds.

He sketched wings bound for air
studied fierce angels
in apocalyptic texts –
how their black feathers faded
to white-tinged yellow
gradually, burnt umber
modulated to dull red
then growing fainter.

                    They could have taken flight
from the vellum margins of a sacred manuscript –
mysterious, Mediaeval – their feet in one world,
wings in quite some other.

And even those of certain butterflies –
the comma, peacock, brimstone, tortoiseshell –
so fine and summer-delicate
are proof against the dark
and damp and cold

as in a blaze of brilliance
from seeming dead
one spreads
his over-wintered wings
and soars.

NOWHERE TO HIDE

The trees are winter-lean.
Without that summer screen
of beech and birch

the giant V (where magpies
flapped and squawked)
is now quite visible –

crotch of a witch
that spawned a tribe of thieves.
Each one that fledged

spelt sorrow
for some small and freckled egg
deep in the ivy or a hawthorn hedge.

UNDERBRUSH

The storm that split your sky is heading north
tonight. You should be here – lightning's
our element: staccato, fork or sheet
flashing from clouds as heaven strikes at earth –
not in the garden, solitary, you,
cider in hand below gaunt sycamores,
mock orange buds, but cautious of those briars
where fox might fire the night. I, on my own –
under the barberry, thorns snagged in my hair
watching dusk dull the glow of buttercups
by still small pools of speedwell – conjuring.
A just-fledged wren lands on a garden chair
small feathery omen from an ivied gloom:
what is there teeming in the underbrush?

CUCKOO PINT

It stalks among
the summer gone to seed

too dangerous
for a suburban garden

the kind of red
a painter, fuelled by wine,

stabs on taut canvas
in a tired room

to the ragged
screech of owls

while branches
of torn oak

grope at
the thatch.

COLDHARBOUR

Names are fluid. In greener days
this was, perhaps, a place where wayfarers
might find a shelter – but no food or fire.

Col d'arbre, on the other hand, could be
simply a ridge of trees.

Whatever, we are walking
toward woods I do not know,
uphill into a gloaming
the day before the year turns.

The path grows steep after
we leave behind

stove-lit stone cottages
cosy with books and chintz

and step among the trees.

You think you know the way –
that there's a tower somewhere at the top.

The last light plays
will o' the wisp in clearings
as we search

and beckons us
into benightedness.

LOVE'S ELASTIC

To distance me (again) you turn your back
as if a blaze in June can be controlled
now love's elastic, strained so, has grown slack.

You claim it's guilt that's cast you on the rack.
How strange it took nine summers to take hold
to distance me. Again you turn. You're back...

My silence helped snow gather on those tracks
where straying feet and straying hearts take cold
and love's elastic's strained and so grows slack.

You run from him, from me. Yourself. Attack
whatever's – almost – close, chasing fool's gold
to distance me. Again you turn your back.

A shaft of sunlight winter cannot hack
kickstarts the thaw's detritus – a threshold
where love's elastic strains and grows more slack.

It's risky to defy the zodiac
to turn and face the future all blindfold
to distance me. Again, you turn your back
and love's elastic's strained and grown too slack.

A YEAR AND A DAY ...

after which time
the serf who's been laid low's
free from his feudal lord;

the pair who lived in sin
can claim the privileges
of those who're wed;

the soul which slipped in death
into the laving waters of a stream
can rise, reborn.

And the knight who's on a quest
must kill the beast,
crack the conundrum,
else...

As such a span of time
has passed since I was touched
by your malevolence

I'm laying claim
to the power of that spell
in casting off a yoke.

LIVING IN THE MOMENT

Whenever we'd visited some far-flung place
at the top of your current whim list, no matter how taken
        you'd been
with swallows diving on faded wallpaper in a decaying state
        room,
warm-walled kitchen gardens, a hidden ice house,
ha-ha or revolving writing shed
you would announce,
We'll never go there again.

I used to say it for you as a joke.
Ticked off, I'd muse
on deep green secrets
the grounds might keep
till autumn stripped them bare.
What snow would make of it.

The moment's passed. Another phrase
I'd baulk at when, in spite of sibilance,
it fell, deadweight, however light the mood.

Whenever I hear it, I think of that time
snatched in a café somewhere at King's Cross,
when you said if we'd met
in circumstances other
than we did …

That moment's passed.
But I wonder sometimes
if you ever go there.

GINNEL

(i) *The Space Between*

Ginnel, ennog, alleyway
jetty, jitty, vennel
snicket, tewer, gulley, chare
passage, wynd or gennel?

(ii) *Collage*

The early sun can't make it
down the ginnel

that runs north from the main road to
an 80s cul-de-sac. So ice

is ice for longer. Today

the giant pockmark
in the unkempt tarmac
is smoothed by it:
                a living Braque
all glittering facet
angular prismatic

over haphazard leaves – ivy
torn sycamore

a smattering
of hawthorn.

An installation
courtesy of cold

remnants of autumn
in a shifting frame.

(iii) *Rib*

The closed-in scent is rank
though has a certain sweetness. Bluebells
are past their chime. Someone has tried

to strip the ivy off a wooden fence,
but, like the torso of an ancient beast,
its leafless ribs cling on. While flat

and lacking heart
a dream of Eden
lives in each grey bone.

(iv) *The Lovers*

I come upon them from the south.
Today the scene could be a Tarot card:

a girl and boy who're crouching face to face,
absorbed. I have to step around them.

Cypress and holly arch in green union
of leaf and branch and twig above their heads

while opportunists – bindweed, snaking ivy –
creep through the failing fence; last autumn's

leaves lie brown along the sides although it's nearly Beltane;
nearby, the broken eggshell of a dove.

I do not glance behind, but know the sun
will frame the entrance as it's moving west.

(v) ... *and the Wardrobe*

Left to themselves, bindweed and ivy and their straggly crew
would make short work of tarmac, of weathered timber. Though
every now and then the council intervenes
to strip or spray each straying green,

time is irrelevant. It's written
in the pink stars of Herb Robert
how that rotting kick board
will soon detach. A tiny leaf turns

as if by magic on spider invisibles
and maybe, through that jigsaw gap,
spanning at least three boards, some children
charmed by Narnia

will find a doorway.

(vi) *Silver*

All along the fence lean lanky plants
which, by their very stance
(despite dark leaves like elongated hearts)
let it be known they're weeds.

Their yellow flowers are mean for their size
too pale to pass as gold. And it annoys me that
they don't quite match an illustration
in my pocket guide, so I can't name them.

There's litter on the ground
and a fetid scent of pent-up afternoon
but a night visitor who is long gone
has crossed my path with silver.

(vii) *Being Watched*

Stalks of honesty
have cashed in purple
for newly minted coin;

sluttish rosebay leans
toward passers-by –
twirls seed into the air;

above my head
cypress and damson
interweave

while a white cat
sails by my feet, slinks up
the left-hand fence

regards me from
the vantage of a shed
through ivy and unnerving

yellow eyes.

(vii) *Seventy-seven Steps*

Here

my footfalls
have a different energy

shadow and green
create a synergy

and I discover
(numerologically)

that seven stands
for magicality.

CUCKOO SPIT

On squally nights, under
the rolling quilt, she thinks of it:

foaming on blades
of long grass in the park,

in the ragged hawthorn copse
at Spuggy's Arch and the verge

beside the ditch in Moor Lane:
each one a random sud of bubble wrap,

a small grub, at its centre,
green and safe.

WAYWARD

Night will be mine
when I dispense
with the set names
of the stars:

maybe I'll reinstate
some of those constellations lost to us –
forged in the minds
of old astronomers –

Apis and Cerberus
Felis, Noctua –

bright chains
which burst their links
fading from view

when some celestial cartographer
re-scripted the sky.

Like the child
scorning the numbers
of a dot to dot

I will ignore the lore
make free with light

unbelt Orion
restring the old lyre

so destiny
is dancing
to my tune.

THE LOST ART OF PATIENCE

Despite a bleak forecast
the March sun holds its own.
There's only me on the steps

of the orangery, watching two crows
competing for a mate against
the backdrop of the Italian Garden.

Each male puffs up neck feathers
prances, struts – with an urgency
that's verging on burlesque.

Such a raucous love triangle –
the rival suitors in a desperate flap
as the object of affection vacillates.

A robin perches on a huge stone urn.
Billows of yew hedge, dulled to verdigris,
are starred by bright new growth.

While strewn on path and lawn,
or under briars in the wilderness, pine cones
(seeds sealed by scales) lie low and wait.

THE PLAGUE DOCTOR OF HELLESDON

The police felt obliged to issue a warning.
A member of the public had complained –
thought children would be scared
and her own mother was afraid of masks…

But in the picture he spelt Gravitas.
That grey-beaked head conjured an underworld
where half-bird furies persecute the damned.
And whether it was filled with ambergris, rose petals,
camphor, juniper or mint, it spoke of otherness:

a figure of doom that might herald a cure.

Moroccan leather boots
tread on stale straw;
the leather gown is waxed
so nothing sticks;
a wide-brimmed hat sits
over eyes of glass
as proof against miasma. Charms
written out in blood.
Spiders and toads to suck up the bad air.
A pole to enforce distance

… commanding more respect
than barefaced hordes
in search of what won't perish
raiding near-empty aisles.

THE AUNT WHO NEVER WAS

Bywell Road looped away
from the main street.

Her wooden greenhouse
with the yellow smell
bristled with cacti.

Over the hearth
hung the frieze
of a naked youth
festooned with grapes –
Bacchus or Dionysus dallying.

Laura, the parrot from the Amazon,
shed rainforest feathers
all blue-green
across the sink-down sofa.

An abstract,
Fighting Cocks, fireball
of red and gold
screamed murder
from the wall.

She made a noise
from the back of her throat
like a wren.

Left the bathroom window
wide all summer when
two blackbirds built a nest there.

Once, on holiday,
she kept an owl awake

all afternoon
by lobbing stones
up to the canopy
so it would be too tired
to hunt by night.

She wasn't of my blood
despite the way I'd been told
to address her.

But as I turn each page –
the first inscribed
in sepia copperplate –
she flutters from the leaves
of *My Brimful Book*
and I sense the current shift.

VISITING TIME

(i) Short Back and Sides

They have cut your hair. Strangely.
You look younger and I'm reminded

of that photo – you in gunner's uniform
before the prison camp. You are

my dad and not my dad as you
ask again about the brother

I don't have. Flinch when fireworks
explode as gunfire

and Singapore falls once more
in a small market town this November.

(ii) Losing It

Your old Rotary watch is still in my pocket
– the staff were worried you would lose the pieces.

These days, you take things that don't work
to bits. And nothing works.

They have forgotten you are left-handed.
You grope for time strapped

to the wrong wrist. On the cheap replacement
Roman numerals conspire

against you, alien as chopsticks
to unpractised hands.

SHARING A RIDE

He seemed to love them more as his world shrank
from wheels to jumbled print.

They starred the small front garden every summer:
noon-flowers unveiling otherworldly colours
pale yellow, orange-pink, all shades of mauve.

It's been ten years. I'm drawn to buy some seeds –
Mixed Sparkles? Harlequin? Maybe the mix whose name
conjures up thoughts of *The Arabian Nights*?

I make my choice – do what that packet says –
and when midsummer dawns
a magic carpet's spread before my feet

each shut bloom coaxed by the June sun's bright wand
into a fabric from a fairy-tale.

I take a step.

PATHETIC FALLACY

After an April that has, so far, eschewed
eponymous showers in favour of full-on sun
Tuesday rolls up cold and grey and bleak.

Ahead, Gonerby's church spire is muted
by drizzle, while, to the left, in the not-now field
sprawls the raw red sameness of yet more new-build.

And I'm aware how moods this lockdown Spring
are lifted by sun, damped down by rain. Had it been
bright, dry underfoot, I might be thinking

that Queen Anne's lace is the tallest hedgerow flower.
But today it's cow parsley at best, and, given the fact
my boots have let in water – and darkening jeans

are flapping at my ankles, keck's curt consonance
is sounding the right tune.
                              But wait – each stem

leans from the grasses pearled with morning rain
while tiny globes of hawthorn buds even now
unclench pale blooms

anticipating May.

LAMMASTIDE

Dancing or duelling
with a fey east wind
barley shows its backbone

bows and flexes
from green
to rippling silver.

It's willing me
to wade into its heart –
but who could brave those waves
and keep her head?

To stay upright
I focus on the sky.
A buzzard floats above
then slips the eye.

Ahead the path dissolves.

THE NAMES OF GRASSES

susurrate on my tongue –

cock's-foot, false brome,
sheep's fescue, crested dog's tail.

Hard to discern
the niceties
of one blade from another –

so understated, delicate,
their flowerings
go unpraised.

They waive
such passings-over
gracefully.

But on a blue
and sun-bright July day
on a road to anywhere

your way might be obscured
by Yorkshire fog
purpling swathes
of wasteland

fringing the paths
through wheat and barley fields

while timothy nods from the verge.

THE GREENWOOD SPEAKS:
TWELVE TREES OF OGHAM

Birch

Drive out the spirit

  of the old year

    with a broom of birch

   when sap is rising

in each leafless fountain

    (each shining one, Lady of the Woods)

      stirring in the grove

   send out your arrows

bitch-shafted

   at Beltane sow the seed

      sailing toward the future

   in a boat that is water-sound

Rowan

On a rowan wheel, spin life's thread.
Drive your sheep through a rowan hoop.
To keep a ghost from wandering,
with berried branches stake the dead.

Deck your milk shed with white flowers.
Guard your boat from the whip of the wave
and the door of your house with a rowan sprig.
Carve your runes on a rowan stave.

Alder

The tree of Bran, whose severed head,
for seven long years, kept singing

beside that river which all men must cross
(a bridge between the now and what's to come)

echoed by ravens in the topmost branches
among the purple leaf buds, royal colours.

When alder's felled its sanctity's made plain:
as white wood seems to bleed.

Willow

Willows bow low;
their leaves dance
in a rhythmic to-and-fro

to the wind's whim – show
silver like the moon
turning pale undersides. Echo

her face which, in the darkening undertow,
lies deep as history on those tides
which heave below.

Ash

It's said Yggdrasil –
from which the god Odin
hung nine long days,

while he absorbed
the secret lore
of those three worlds
it spanned, from roots
to topmost branch –
was an ash tree

just as it's said
that ash invites
the illumination
of a lightning strike.

It's said the seeds
are keys.

Pluck one –
find where it fits
in the wide trunk.

Hawthorn

When its whites
herald the light
half of the year
spring singing
in the hedge

harness the power
of the rising sun
pick blossom
to weave garlands
for the maypole

and, as the earth is pulsing,

cut swathes of foaming
heady-scented whitethorn,

to deck the bower
of the Beltane bride.

Oak

Chosen to host mistletoe,
seed of the gods,
which falls from heaven
on the forest king.

Chosen for lightning
by the thunderer –
a channel leading from
his realm to earth.

Struck, it regenerates.

Even in death,
branches twist skyward

like the antler crown

of the wild hunter Herne.
He chose this tree
to house his fearsome spirit.

Holly

(i)

As days grow short
holly is radiant:
his glossy leaves reflect

a weakening sun
while flame-red berries
pricked on evergreen

ignite the winter woods
keep dark

at bay.

(ii)

Holly burns hot – the heart
of the smith's forge where he

will mould the elements
and so perfect

the magic of his brand
of alchemy.

Hazel

Loved by him whose wand of hazel
is entwined by sinuous serpents

prized by druids and by dowsers
who divine the springs of wisdom:

fat with knowledge are the salmon
pliant as the hazel branches

which overhang the well of Connla
let their fruits fall in the waters.

Thoughts move swiftly as quicksilver
through the minds of those who eat them.

Apple

From his great master Gwendolleu
Merlin learned of the orchard:
seven score times seven trees

all guarded by two birds
with dusky feathers
and wearing yokes of gold.

On all his journeyings
he could create
this same enchanted place
a healing space.

The blood red apple of the sun
sinks low at night
but rises, always,
radiating light.

Ivy

Ivy blooms in autumn,
        its greenish-yellow umbels
a rich, late trove of nectar for the bees;

        its berries, ripe in winter,
see birds through until spring.

Weaver of time and fate, Arianrhod,
        Celtic goddess of the silver wheel,
claimed ivy as her own.

        Behind its veil of green
the dusty moths make home.

Elder

The ancient Celts
held faith in the sacred Cauldron of Rebirth
where warriors slain in battle
were immersed,
emerging with their life
and strength
restored.

Close by this vessel
grows the elder tree.

Snap off a branch and see
that from the wound, in time,
new growth
will shoot.

Pushed down into the earth
the smallest twig takes root.

WOODS SEEN FROM A TRAIN

There is something about woods
seen from a train, on which a lone fox
might set his sights, trotting slantwise
across the frozen field:

huddles of trees,
always in circles, always
in the middle of nowhere:

dark cabals
full of old knowings.

And you, too, long
to slip beneath branches
drawn to the heartwood
of a green deep place

but this one is already
behind you as you speed past.

LOSING THE PLOT

She thought
him flawless

but fell
for story

after story
after story

clutching
at denouement.